The Duty of Disobedience

LYDIA MARIA CHILD

Boston 1860

TABLE OF CONTENTS

MOTTO

"Thou shalt not deliver unto his master the servant which is escaped from his master unto thee."—DEUT. 23:15.

APPEAL TO THE LEGISLATORS OF MASSACHUSETTS

I feel there is no need of apologizing to the Legislature of Massachusetts because a woman addresses them. Sir Walter Scott says: "The truth of Heaven was never committed to a tongue, however feeble, but it gave a right to that tongue to announce mercy, while it declared judgment." And in view of all that women have done, and are doing, intellectually and morally, for the advancement of the world, I presume no enlightened legislator will be disposed to deny that the "truth of Heaven" is often committed to them, and that they sometimes utter it with a degree of power that greatly influences the age in which they live.

I therefore offer no excuses on that score. But I do feel as if it required some apology to attempt to convince men of ordinary humanity and common sense that the Fugitive Slave Bill is utterly wicked, and consequently ought never to be obeyed. Yet Massachusetts consents to that law! Some shadow of justice she grants, inasmuch as her Legislature have passed what is called a Personal Liberty Bill, securing trial by jury to those claimed as slaves. Certainly it is something gained, especially for those who may get brown by working in the sunshine, to prevent our Southern masters from taking any of us, at a moment's notice, and dragging us off into perpetual bondage. It is something gained to require legal proof that a man is a slave, before he is given up to arbitrary torture and unrecompensed toil. But is that the measure of justice becoming the character of a free Commonwealth? "Prove that the man is property, according your laws, and I will drive him into your cattle-pen with sword and bayonet," is what Massachusetts practically says to Southern tyrants. "Show me a Bill of Sale from the Almighty!" is what she ought to say. No other proof should be considered valid in a Christian country.

One thousand five hundred years ago, Gregory, a Bishop in Asia Minor, preached a sermon in which he rebuked the sin of slaveholding. Indignantly he asked, "Who can be the possessor of human beings save God? Those men that you say belong to you, did not God create them free? Command the brute creation; that is well. Bend the beasts of the field beneath your yoke. But are your fellow-men to be bought and sold, like herds of cattle? Who can pay the value of a being created in the image of God? The whole world itself bears no proportion to the value of a soul, on which the Most High has set the seal his likeness. This world will perish, but the soul of man is immortal. Show me, then, your titles of possession. Tell me whence you derive this strange claim. Is not your own nature the same with that of those you call your slaves? Have they not the same origin with yourselves? Are they not born to the same immortal destinies?"

Thus spake a good old Bishop, in the early years of Christianity. Since then, thousands and thousands of noble souls have given their bodies to the gibbet and the stake, to help onward the slow progress of truth and freedom; a great unknown continent has been opened as a new, free starting point for the human race; printing has been invented, and the command, "Whatsoever ye would that men should do unto you, do ye even so unto them," has been sent abroad in all the languages of the earth. And here, in the noon-day light the nineteenth century, in a nation claiming to be the freest and most enlightened on the face of the globe, a portion the population of fifteen States have thus agreed among themselves: "Other men shall work for us, without wages while we smoke, and drink, and gamble, and race horses, and fight. We will have their wives and daughters for concubines, and sell their children in the market with horses and pigs. If they make any objection to this arrangement, we will break them into subjection with the cow-hide and the bucking-paddle. They shall not be permitted to read or write, because that would be likely to 'produce dissatisfaction in their minds.' If they attempt to run away from us, our blood-hounds shall tear the flesh from their bones, and any man who sees them may shoot them down like mad dogs. If they succeed in getting beyond our frontier, into States where it is the custom to pay men for their work, and to protect their wives and children from outrage, we will compel the people of those States to drive them back into the jaws of our blood-hounds."

And what do the people of the other eighteen States of that enlightened country answer to this monstrous demand? What says Massachusetts, with the free blood of the Puritans coursing in her veins, and with the sword uplifted in her right hand, to procure "peaceful repose under liberty"? Massachusetts answers: "O yes. We will be your blood-hounds, and pay our own expenses. Only prove to our satisfaction that the stranger who has taken refuge among us is one of the men you have agreed among yourselves to whip into working without wages, and we will hunt him back for you. Only prove to us that this woman, who has run away from your harem, was bought for a concubine, that you might get more drinking-money by the sale of the children she bears you, and our soldiers will hunt her back with alacrity."

Shame on my native State! Everlasting shame! Blot out the escutcheon of the brave old Commonwealth! Instead of the sword uplifted to protect liberty, let the slave-driver's whip be suspended over a blood-hound, and take for your motto, Obedience to tyrants is the highest law.

Legislators of Massachusetts, can it be that you really understand what Slavery is, and yet consent that a fugitive slave, who seeks protection here, shall be driven back to that dismal house of bondage? For sweet charity's sake, I must suppose that you have been too busy with your farms and your merchandise ever to have imagined yourself in the situation of a slave. Let me suppose a case for you; one of a class of cases occurring by hundreds every year. Suppose your father was Governor of Carolina and your mother was a slave. The Governor's wife hates your mother, and is ingenious in inventing occasions to have you whipped. You don't know the reason why, poor child! but your mother knows full well. If they would only allow her to go away and work for wages, she would gladly toil and earn money to buy you. But that your father will not allow. His laws have settled it that she is his property, "for all purposes whatsoever," and he will keep her as long as suits his convenience. The mistress continually insists upon her being sold far away South; and after a while, she has her will. Your poor mother clings to you convulsively; but the slave-driver gives you both a cut of his whip, and tells you to stop your squalling. They drive her off with the gang, and you never hear of her again; but, for a long time afterward, it makes you very sad to remember the farewell look of those large, loving eyes. Your poor mother had handsome eyes; and that was one reason her mistress hated her.

You also are your father's property; and when he dies, you will be the property of your whiter brother. You black his shoes, tend upon him at table, and sleep on the floor in his room, to give him water if he is thirsty in the night. You see him learning to read, and you hear your father read wonderful things from the newspapers. Very naturally, you want to read, too. You ask your brother to teach you the letters. He gives you a kick, calls you a "damned nig," and informs his father, who orders you to be flogged for insolence. Alone on the hard floor at night, still smarting from your blows, you ponder over the great mystery of knowledge and wonder why it would do you any more harm than it does your brother. Henceforth, all scraps of newspapers you can find are carefully laid by. Helplessly you pore over them, at stolen moments, as if you expected some miracle would reveal the meaning of those printed signs. Cunning comes to your aid. It is the only weapon of the weak against the strong. When you see white boys playing in the street, you trace a letter in the sand, and say, "My young master calls that B." "That ain't B, you dammed nigger. That's A"! they shout. Now you know what shape is A; and diligently you hunt it out wherever it is to be found on your scraps of newspaper. By slow degrees you toil on, in similar ways, through all the alphabet. No student of Greek or Hebrew ever deserved so much praise for ingenuity and diligence. But the years pass on, and still you cannot read. Your master-brother now and then gives you a copper. You hoard them, and buy a primer; screening yourself from suspicion, by telling the bookseller that your master wants it for his sister's little boy. You find the picture of a cat, with three letters by its side; and now you know how cat is spelt. Elated with your wonderful discovery, you are eager to catch a minute to study your primer. Too eager, alas! for your mistress catches you absorbed in it, and your little book is promptly burned. You are sent to be flogged, and your lacerated back is washed with brine to make it heal quickly. But in spite of all their efforts, your intelligent mind is too cunning for them. Before twenty years have passed, you have stumbled along into the Bible; alone in the dark, over a rugged road of vowels and consonants. You keep the precious volume concealed under a board in the floor, and read it at snatches, by the light of a pine knot. You read that God has created of one blood all the nations of the earth; and that his commandment is, to do unto others as we would that they should do unto us. You think of your weeping mother, torn from your tender arms by the cruel slave-trader; of the interdicted light of knowledge; of the Bible kept as a sealed book from all whose skins have a tinge of black, or brown, or yellow; of how those brown and yellow complexions came to be so common; of yourself, the son of the Governor, yet obliged to read the Bible by stealth, under the penalty of a bleeding back washed with brine. These and many other things revolve in your active mind, and your unwritten inferences are worth whole folios of theological commentaries.

As youth ripens into manhood, life bears for you, as it does for others, its brightest, sweetest flower. You love young Amy, with rippling black hair, and large dark eyes, with long, silky fringes. You inherit from your father, the Governor, a taste for beauty warmly-tinted, like Cleopatra's. You and Amy are of rank to make a suitable match; for you are the son of a Southern Governor, and she is the daughter of a United States Senator, from the North, who often shared her master's hospitality; her handsome mother being a portion of that hospitality, and he being large-minded enough to "conquer prejudices." You have good sympathy in other respects also, for your mothers were both slaves; and as it is conveniently and profitably arranged for the masters that "the child shall follow the condition of the mother," you are consequently both of you slaves. But there are some compensations for your hard lot. Amy's simple admiration flatters your vanity. She considers you a prodigy of learning because you can read the Bible, and she has not the faintest idea how such skill can be acquired. She gives you her whole heart, full of the blind confidence of a first love. The divine spark, which kindles aspirations for freedom in the human soul, has been glowing more and more brightly since you have emerged from boyhood, and now her glances kindle it into a flame. For her dear sake, you long to be a free man, with power to protect her from the degrading incidents of a slave-girl's life. Wages acquire new value in your eyes, from a wish to supply her with comforts, and enhance her beauty by becoming dress. For her sake, you are ambitious to acquire skill in the carpenter's trade, to which your, master-brother has applied you as the best investment of his human capital. It is true, he takes all your wages; but then, by acquiring uncommon facility, you hope to accomplish your daily tasks in shorter time, and thus obtain some extra hours to do jobs for yourself. These you can eke out by working late into the night, and rising when the day dawns. Thus you calculate to be able in time to buy the use of your own limbs. Poor fellow! Your intelligence and industry prove a misfortune. They charge twice as much for the machine of your body on account of the soul-power which moves it. Your master-brother tells you that you would bring eighteen hundred dollars in the market. It is a large sum. Almost hopeless seems the prospect of earning it, at such odd hours as you can catch when the hard day's task is done. But you look at Amy, and are inspired with faith to remove mountains. Your master-brother graciously consents to receive payment by instalments. These prove a convenient addition to the whole of your wages. They will enable him to buy a new race horse, and increase his stock of choice wines. While he sleeps off drunkenness, you are toiling for him, with the blessed prospect of freedom far ahead, but burning brightly in the distance, like a Drummond Light, guiding the watchful mariner over a midnight sea.

When you have paid five hundred dollars of the required sum, your lonely heart so longs for the comforts of a home, that you can wait no longer. You marry Amy, with the resolution of buying her also, and removing to those Free States, about which you have often talked together, as invalids discourse of heaven. Amy is a member of the church, and it is a great point with her to be married by a minister. Her master and mistress make no objection, knowing that after the ceremony, she will remain an article of property, the same as ever. Now come happy months, during which you almost forget that you are a slave, and that it must be a weary long while before you can earn enough to buy yourself and your dear one, in addition to supporting your dissipated master. But you toil bravely on, and soon pay another hundred dollars toward your ransom. The Drummond Light of Freedom burns brighter in the diminished distance.

Alas! in an unlucky hour, your tipsy master-brother sees your gentle Amy, and becomes enamored of her large dark eyes, and the rich golden tint of her complexion. Your earnings and your ransom-money make him flush of cash. In spite of all your efforts to prevent it, she becomes his property. He threatens to cowhide you, if you ever speak to her again. You remind him that she is your wife; that you were married by a minister. "Married, you damned nigger!" he exclaims; "what does a slave's marriage amount to? If you give me any more of your insolence, you'll get a taste of the cowhide."

Anxious days and desolate nights pass. There is such a heavy pain at your heart, it is a mystery to yourself that you do not die. At last, Amy contrives to meet you, pale and wretched as yourself. She has a mournful story to tell of degrading propositions, and terrible threats. She promises to love you always, and be faithful to you till death, come what may. Poor Amy! When she said that, she did not realize how powerless is the slave, in the hands of an unprincipled master. Your interview was watched, and while you were sobbing in each other's arms, you were seized and ordered to receive a hundred lashes. While you are lying in jail, stiff with your wounds, your master-brother comes to tell you he has sold you to a trader from Arkansas. You remind him of the receipt he has given you for six hundred dollars, and ask him to return the money. He laughs in your face, and tells you his receipt is worth no more than so much brown paper; that no contracts with a slave are binding. He coolly adds, "Besides, it has taken all my spare money to buy Amy." Perhaps you would have killed him in that moment of desperation, even with the certainty of being burnt to cinders for the deed, but you are too horribly wounded by the lash to be able to spring upon him. In that helpless condition, you are manacled and carried off by the slave-trader. Never again will Amy's gentle eyes look into yours. What she suffers you will never know. She is suddenly wrenched from your youth, as your mother was from your childhood. The pall of silence falls over all her future. She cannot read or write; and the post-office was not instituted for slaves.

Looking back on that dark period of desolation and despair, you marvel how you lived through it. But the nature of youth is elastic. You have learned that law offers colored men nothing but its penalties; that white men engross all its protection; still you are tempted to make another bargain for your freedom. Your new master seems easy and good-natured, and you trust he will prove more honorable than your brother has been. Perhaps he would; but unfortunately, he is fond of cards; and when you have paid him two hundred dollars, he stakes them, and you also, at the gaming-table, and loses. The winner is a hard man, noted for severity to his slaves. Now you resolve to take the risk of running away, with all its horrible chances. You hide in a neighboring swamp, where you are bitten by a venomous snake, and your swollen limb becomes almost incapable of motion. In great anguish, you drag it along, through the midnight darkness, to the hut of a poor plantation-slave, who binds on a poultice of ashes, but dares not, for fear of his life, shelter you after day has dawned. He helps you to a deep gully, and there you remain till evening, half-famished for food. A man in the neighborhood keeps blood-hounds, well trained to hunt runaways. They get on your track, and tear flesh from the leg which the snake had spared. To escape them, you leap into the river. The sharp ring of rifles meets your ear. You plunge under water. When you come up to take breath, a rifle ball lodges in your shoulder and you plunge again. Suddenly, thick clouds throw their friendly veil over the moon. You swim for your life, with balls whizzing round you. Thanks to the darkness and the water, you baffle the hounds, both animal and human. Weary and wounded, you travel through the forests, your eye fixed hopefully on the North Star, which seems ever beckoning you onward to freedom, with its bright glances through the foliage. In the day-time, you lie in the deep holes of swamps, concealed by rank weeds and tangled vines, taking such rest as can be obtained among swarms of mosquitoes and snakes. Through incredible perils and fatigues, footsore and emaciated, you arrive at last in the States called Free. You allow yourself little time to rest, so eager are you to press on further North. You have heard the masters swear with peculiar violence about Massachusetts, and you draw the inference that it is a refuge for the oppressed. Within the borders of that old Commonwealth, you breathe more freely than you have ever done. You resolve to rest awhile, at least, before you go to Canada. You find friends, and begin to hope that you may be allowed to remain and work, if you prove yourself industrious and well behaved. Suddenly, you find yourself arrested and chained. Soldiers escort you through the streets of Boston, and put you on board a Southern ship, to be sent back to your master. When you arrive, he orders you to be flogged so unmercifully, that the doctor says you will die if they strike another blow. The philanthropic city of Boston hears the bloody tidings, and one of her men in authority says to the public: "Fugitive slaves are a class of foreigners, with whose rights Massachusetts has nothing to do. It is enough for us, that they have no right to be here."[1] And the merchants of Boston cry, Amen.

[1] Said by the U.S. Commissioner, George Ticknor Curtis, at a Union Meeting, in the Old Cradle of Liberty.

Legislators of Massachusetts! if you had been thus continually robbed of your rights by the hand of violence, what would you think of the compact between North and South to perpetuate your wrongs, and transmit them to your posterity? Would you not regard it as a league between highwaymen, who had "no rights that you were bound to respect"? I put the question plainly and directly to your consciences and your common sense, and they will not allow you to answer, No. Are you, then, doing right to sustain the validity of a law for others, which you would vehemently reject for yourselves in the name of outraged justice and humanity?

The incidents I have supposed might happen to yourselves if you were slaves, are not an imaginary accumulation of horrors. The things I have described are happening in this country every day. I have talked with many "fugitives from injustice," and I could not, within the limits of these pages, even hint at a tithe of the sufferings and wrongs they have described. I have also talked with several slaveholders, who had emancipated themselves from the hateful system. Being at a safe distance from lynching neighbors, they could venture to tell the truth; and their statements fully confirm all that I have heard from the lips of slaves. If you read Southern Laws, you will need very small knowledge of human nature to be convinced that the practical results must inevitably be utter barbarism. In view of those laws, I have always wondered how sensible people could be so slow in believing the actual state of things in slaveholding communities.

There are no incidents in history, or romance, more thrilling than the sufferings, perils, and hair-breadth escapes of American slaves. No Puritan pilgrim, or hero of '76, has manifested more courage and perseverance in the cause of freedom, than has been evinced, in thousands of instances, by this persecuted race. In future ages, popular ballads will be sung to commemorate their heroic achievements, and children more enlightened than ours will marvel at the tyranny of their white ancestors.

All of you have doubtless read some accounts of what these unhappy men and women have dared and endured. Did you never put yourselves in their stead, and imagine how you would feel, under similar circumstances? Not long ago, a young man escaped from slavery by clinging night and day to the under part of a steamboat, drenched by water, and suffering for food. He was discovered and sent back. If the Constitution of the United States sanctioned such an outrage upon you, what would you think of those who answered your entreaties and remonstrances by saying, "Our fathers made an agreement with the man who robs you of your wages and your freedom. It is law; and it is your duty to submit to [Transcriber's note: word cut off] patiently"? I think you would then perceive the necessity of having the Constitution forthwith amended; and if it were not done very promptly, I apprehend you would appeal vociferously to a higher law.

A respectable lady, who removed with her family from Virginia to New York, some years ago, had occasion to visit the cook's cabin, to prepare suitable nourishment for a sick child, during the voyage. This is the story she tells: "The steward kindly assisted me in making the toast, and added a cracker and a cup of tea. With these on a small waiter, I was returning to the cabin, when, in passing the freight, which consisted of boxes, bags, etc., a little tawny, famished-looking hand was thrust out between the packages. The skeleton fingers, agitated by a convulsive movement, were evidently reached forth to obtain the food. Shocked, but not alarmed by the apparition, I laid the cracker on the hand, which was immediately withdrawn. No one observed the transaction, and I went swiftly to the cabin. In the afternoon, I went to the steward again, in behalf of the little invalid. Finding he was a father, I gave him presents for his children, and so ingratiated myself into his favor, that I had free access to the larder. Whatever I could procure, I divided with the famished hand, which had become to me a precious charge. As all was tranquil on board, it was evident that I alone was aware of the presence of the fugitive. I humbly returned thanks to God for the privilege of ministering to the wants of this his outcast, despised and persecuted image. That the unfortunate being was a slave, I doubted not. I knew the laws and usages in such cases. I knew the poor creature had nothing to expect from the captain or crew; and again and again I asked myself the agonizing question whether there would be any way of escape. I hoped we should arrive in the night, that the fugitive might go on shore unseen, under favor of the darkness. I determined to watch and assist the creature thus providentially committed to my charge. We had a long passage. On the sixth day, I found that the goods were being moved to come at something which was wanted. My heart seemed to die within me; for the safety of the sufferer had become dear to me. When we sat down to dinner, the dishes swam before my eyes. The tumbling of the freight had not ceased. I felt that a discovery must take place. At length, I heard sudden, Hallo! Presently, the steward came and whispered the captain, who laid down his knife and fork, and went on deck. One of the passengers followed him, but soon returned In a laughing manner, he told us that a small mulatto boy; who said he belonged to Mr. ———, of Norfolk, had been found among the freight. He had been concealed among the lumber on wharves for two weeks, and had secreted himself in the schooner the night before we sailed. He was going to New York, to find his father, who had escaped two years before. 'He is starved to a skeleton,' said he, 'and is hardly worth taking back.' Many jokes were passed as to the manner of his being renovated, when he should fall into the hands of his master.

"The unfortunate child was brought on deck, and we all left the cabin to look at him. I stood some time in the companion-way before I could gain strength to move forward. As soon as he discovered me, a bright gleam passed over his countenance, and he instantly held out to me that famished hand. My feelings could no longer be controlled. There stood before me a child, not more than eleven or twelve years of age, of yellow complexion, and a sad countenance. He was nearly naked; his back was seared with scars, and his flesh was wasted to the bone. I burst into tears, and the jeers of others were for a moment changed into sympathies. It began, however, to be suspected that I had brought the boy away; and in that case, the vessel must put back, in order to give me up also. But I related the circumstances, and all seemed satisfied with the truth of my statement.

"I asked to be allowed to feed the boy, and the request was granted. He ate voraciously, and, as I stood beside him, he looked into my face at every mouthful. There was something confiding in his look. When he had finished his meal, as I took the plate, he rubbed his fingers softly on my hand, and leaned his head toward me, like a weary child. O that I could have offered him a place of rest! that I could have comforted and protected him! a helpless child! a feeble, emaciated, suffering, innocent child, reserved for bondage and torture!

"The captain informed us that the vessel had been forbidden to enter the port with a fugitive slave on board. He must discharge her cargo where she lay, and return, with all possible dispatch, to Norfolk. Accordingly, we came to anchor below the city, and the passengers were sent up in a boat, I said to the captain, 'There is a great ado about a poor helpless child.' He replied, 'The laws must be obeyed.' I could not help exclaiming, 'Is this the land of boasted freedom?' Here was an innocent child treated like a felon; manacled, and sent back to slavery and the lash; deprived of the fostering care which even the brute is allowed to exercise toward its young. The slender boy was seeking the protection of a father. Did humanity aid him? No. Humanity was prevented by the law, which consigns one portion of the people to the control and brutality of the other. Humanity can only look on and weep. 'The laws must be obeyed.'"

Legislators of Massachusetts! suppose for one moment that poor abused boy was your own little Johnny or Charley, what would you say of the law then? Truly, if we have no feeling for the children of others, we deserve to have our own children reserved for such a fate; and I sometimes think it is the only lesson that will teach the North to respect justice and humanity.

It is not long ago, since a free colored man in Baltimore was betrothed to a young slave of eighteen, nearly white, and very beautiful. If they married, their children would be slaves, and he would have no power to protect his handsome wife from any outrages an unprincipled master, or his sons, might choose to perpetrate. Therefore, he wisely resolved to marry in a land of freedom. He placed her in a box, with a few holes in it, small enough not to attract attention. With tender care, he packed hay around her, that she might not be bruised when thrown from the cars with other luggage. The anxiety of the lover was dreadful. Still more terrible was it, when waiting for her in Philadelphia, he found that the precious box had not arrived. They had happened to have an unusual quantity of freight, and the baggage-master, after turning the box over, in rough, railroad fashion had concluded to leave it till the next train. The poor girl was thrown into a most uneasy position, without the power of changing it. She was nearly suffocated for want of air; the hay-seed fell into her eyes and nostrils, and it required almost superhuman efforts to refrain from sneezing or choking. Added to this was terror lest her absence be discovered, and the heavy box examined. In that state of mind and body, she remained more than two hours, in the hot sun on the railroad platform. At last, the box arrived in Philadelphia, and the lover and his friends conveyed it to a place of safety as speedily as possible. Those who were present at the opening, say it was the most impressive scene they ever witnessed. Silently, almost breathlessly, they drew out the nails, expecting to find a corpse. When the cover was lifted, she smiled faintly in the anxious face of her lover. "O God, she is alive!" he exclaimed, and broke down in a paroxysm of sobs. She had a terrible brain fever, and when she recovered from it, her glossy hair was sprinkled with gray, and the weight of ten years was added to her youthful face. Thanks to the vigilance and secrecy of friends, the hounds of the United States, who use the Constitution for their kennel, did not get a chance to lap the blood of this poor trembling hare.

Legislators of Massachusetts! suppose this innocent girl had been your own Mary or Emma, would you not straightway demand amendment of the Constitution, in no very measured terms? And if it could not be obtained right speedily, would you not ride over the Constitution roughshod? If you would not, you do not deserve to have such blessings as lovely and innocent daughters.

You have all heard of Margaret Garner, who escaped from Kentucky to Ohio, with her father and mother, her husband and four children. The Cincinnati papers described her as "a dark mulatto, twenty-three years of age, of an interesting appearance, considerable intelligence, and a good address." Her husband was described as "about twenty-two years old, of a very lithe, active form, and rather a mild, pleasant countenance." These fugitives were sheltered by a colored friend in Ohio. There the hounds in pay of the United States, to which "price of blood" you and I and all of us contribute, ferreted them out, and commanded them to surrender. When they refused to do so, they burst open the door, and assailed the inmates of the house with cudgels and pistols. They defended themselves bravely, but were overpowered by numbers and disarmed. When Margaret perceived that there was no help for her and her little ones, she seized a knife and cut the throat of her most beautiful child. She was about to do the same by the others, when her arm was arrested. The child killed was nearly white, and exceedingly pretty. The others were mulattoes, and pretty also. What history lay behind this difference of complexion, the world will probably never know. But I have talked confidentially with too many fugitive women not to know that very sad histories do lie behind such facts. Margaret Garner knew very well what fate awaited her handsome little daughter, and that nerved her arm to strike the death-blow. It was an act that deserves to take its place in history by the side of the Roman Virginius.

The man who claimed this unfortunate family as chattels acknowledged that they had always been faithful servants. On their part, they complained of cruel treatment from their master, as the cause of their attempt to escape. They were carried to the United States Court, under a strong guard, and there was not manhood enough in Cincinnati to rescue them. What was called law decided that they were property, and they were sent back to the dark dungeon of interminable bondage. The mother could not be induced to express any regret for the death of her child,—her "pretty bird," as she called her. With tears streaming from her eyes, she told of her own toils and sufferings, and said, "It was better they should be killed at once, and end their misery, than to be taken back to slavery, to be murdered by inches." To a preacher, who asked her, "Why did you not trust in God? Why didn't you wait and hope?" she answered, "We did wait; and when there seemed to be no hope for us, we run away. God did not appear to help us, and I did the best I could."

These poor wretches were escorted through the streets by a National Guard, the chivalry of the United States. There was not manhood enough in the Queen City of the West to attempt a rescue; though they are very fond of quoting for themselves, "Give me Liberty, or give me Death!" Men satisfied themselves by saying it was all done according to law. A powerful plea, truly, for a people who boast so much of making their own laws!

These slaves were soon after sent down the Mississippi to be sold in Arkansas. The boat came in collision with another boat, and many were drowned. The shock threw Margaret overboard, with a baby in her arms. She was too valuable a piece of property to lose, and they drew her out of the water; but the baby was gone. She evinced no emotion but joy, still saying it was better for her children to die than to be slaves.

The man who could not afford to let this heroic woman own her little ones, was very liberal in supporting the Gospel, and his wife was a member of the church. Do you think that mother had a murderer's heart? Nay, verily. Exceeding love for her children impelled her to the dreadful deed. The murder was committed by those human hounds, who drove her to that fearful extremity, where she was compelled to choose between Slavery or Death for her innocent offspring.

Again I ask, what would be your judgment of this law, if your own daughter and infant grand-daughter had been its victims? You know very well, that had it been your own case, such despotism, calling itself law, would be swept away in a whirlwind of indignation, and men who strove to enforce it would be obliged to flee the country.

„They are slaves most base, Whose love of right is for themselves, and not for all the race."

I was lately talking with Friend Whittier, whose poetry so stirs the hearts of the people in favor of freedom and humanity. He told me he thought the greatest pain he ever suffered was in witnessing the arrest of a fugitive slave in Philadelphia. The man had lived there many years; he bore a good character, and was thriving by his industry. He had married a Pennsylvania woman, and they had a fine family of children. In the midst of his prosperity and happiness, the blood-hounds of the United States tracked him out. He was seized and hurried into court. Friend Whittier was present, and heard the agonized entreaties of his wife and children. He saw them clinging to the half frantic husband and father, when the minions of a wicked law tore him away from them for ever. That intelligent, worthy, industrious man was ruthlessly plunged into the deep, dark grave of slavery, where tens of thousands perish yearly, and leave no record of their wrongs. "A German emigrant, who witnessed the scene, poured out such a tornado of curses as I never before heard," said Whittier; "and I could not blame the man. He came here supposing America to be a free country, and he was bitterly disappointed. Pity for that poor slave and his bereaved family agonized my heart; and my cheeks burned with shame that my country deserved the red-hot curses of that honest German; but stronger than either of those feelings was overpowering indignation that people of the Free States were compelled by law to witness such barbarities."

Many of you have heard of William and Ellen Crafts, a pious and intelligent couple, who escaped from bondage some years ago. She disguised herself in male attire, and passed for a white gentleman, taking her darker colored husband with her as a servant. When the Fugitive Slave Act went into operation, they received warning that the hounds were on their track. They sought temporary refuge in the house of my noble-hearted friend, Ellis Gray Loring, who then resided in the vicinity of Boston. He and his family were absent for some days; but a lady in the house invited Mr. Crafts to come in and stay till they returned. "No, I thank you," he replied. "There is a heavy fine for sheltering fugitives; and it would not be right to subject Mr. Loring to it without his consent." "But you know he is a true friend to the slaves," urged the lady. "If he were at home, I am sure he would not hesitate to incur the penalty." "Because he is such a good friend to my oppressed race, there is all the more reason why I should not implicate him in my affairs, without his knowledge," replied this nobleman of nature. His wife had slept but little the previous night, having been frightened by dreams of Daniel Webster chasing her husband, pistol in hand. The evening was stormy, and she asked him if they could not remain there till morning. "It would not be right, Ellen," he replied; and with tears in her eyes, they went forth into the darkness and rain. Was that a man to be treated like a chattel? How many white gentlemen are there, who, in circumstances as perilous, would have manifested such nicety of moral perception, such genuine delicacy of feeling? England has kindly received that worthy and persecuted couple. All who set foot on her soil are free. Would to God it were so in Massachusetts!

It is well known that Southerners have repeatedly declared they do not demand fugitives merely to recover articles of property, or for the sake of making an example of them, to inspire terror in other runaways; that they have a still stronger motive, which is, to humiliate the North; to make them feel that no latitude limits their mastership. Have we no honest pride, that we so tamely submit to this? What lethargic disease has fallen on Northern souls, that they dare not be as bold for Freedom as tyrants are for Slavery? It was not thus with our fathers, whose sepulchres we whiten. If old Ben Franklin had stood as near Boston Court House as his statue does, do you believe he would have remained passive, while Sims, the intelligent mechanic, was manacled and driven through the streets, guiltless of any crime, save that of wishing to be free? My belief is that the brave old printer of '76 would have drawn down the lightning out of heaven upon that procession, with a vengeance.

What satisfactory reasons can be alleged for submitting to this degradation? What good excuse can be offered? Shall we resort to the Old Testament argument, that anodyne for the consciences of "South-Side" divines? Suppose the descendants of Ham were ordained to be slaves to the end of time, for an offence committed thousands of years ago, by a progenitor they never heard of. Still, the greatest amount of theological research leaves it very uncertain who the descendants of Ham are, and where they are. I presume you would not consider the title even to one acre of land satisfactorily settled by evidence of such extremely dubious character; how much less, then, a man's ownership of himself! Then, again, if we admit that Africans are descendants of Ham, what is to be said of thousands of slaves, advertised in Southern newspapers as "passing themselves for white men, or white women"? Runaways with "blue eyes, light hair, and rosy complexions"? Are these sons and daughters of our Presidents, our Governors, our Senators, our Generals, and our Commodores, descendants of Ham? Are they Africans?

If you turn to the favorite New Testament argument, you will find that Paul requested Philemon to receive Onesimus, "no longer as a servant, but as a brother beloved." Is that the way Southern masters receive the "fugitives from injustice" whom we drive back to them? Is it the way we expect they will be received? In 1851, the intelligent young mechanic, named Thomas Sims, escaped from a hard master, who gave him many blows and no wages. By his own courage and energy, he succeeded in reaching our Commonwealth, where mechanics are not compelled by law to work without wages. But the authorities of Boston decreed that this man was "bound to such service or labor." So they ordered out their troops and sent him back to his master, who caused him to be tied up and flogged, till the doctor said, "If you strike another blow, you will kill him." "Let him die," replied the master. He did nearly die in prison, but recovered to be sold farther South. Was this being received as "a brother beloved"? Before we send back any more Onesimuses, it is necessary to have a different set of Philemons to deal with. The Scripture is clearly not obeyed, under present circumstances.

If you resort to the alleged legal obligation to return fugitives, it has more plausibility, but has it in reality any firm foundation? Americans boast of making their own laws, and of amending them whenever circumstances render it necessary. How, then, can they excuse themselves, or expect the civilized world to excuse them, for making, or sustaining, unjust and cruel laws? The Fugitive Slave Act has none of the attributes of law. If two highwaymen agreed between themselves to stand by each other in robbing helpless men, women and children, should we not find it hard work to "conquer our prejudices" so far as to dignify their bargain with the name of law? That is the light in which the compact between North and South presents itself to the minds of intelligent slaves, and we should view it in the same way, if we were in their position. Law was established to maintain justice between man and man; and this Act clearly maintains injustice. Law was instituted to protect the weak from the strong; this Act delivers the weak completely into the arbitrary power of the strong, "Law is a rule of conduct, prescribed by the supreme power, commanding what is right, and forbidding what is wrong." This is the commonly received definition of law, and obviously, none more correct could be substituted for it. The application of it would at once annul the Fugitive Slave Act, and abolish slavery. That Act reverses the maxim. It commands what is wrong, and forbids what is right. It commands us to trample on the weak and defenceless, to persecute the oppressed, to be accomplices in defrauding honest laborers of their wages. It forbids us to shelter the homeless, to protect abused innocence, to feed the hungry, to "hide the outcast." Let theological casuists argue as they will, Christian hearts will shrink from thinking of Jesus as surrendering a fugitive slave; or of any of his apostles, unless it be Judas. Political casuists may exercise their skill in making the worse appear the better reason, still all honest minds have an intuitive perception that no human enactment which violates God's laws is worthy of respect. By what law of God can we justify the treatment of Margaret Garner? the surrender of Sims and Burns? the pitiless persecution of that poor little "famished hand"?

There is another consideration, which ought alone to have sufficient weight with us to deter us from attempting to carry out this tyrannical enactment. All history, and all experience, show it to be an immutable law of God, that whosoever injures another, injures himself in the process. These frequent scuffles between despotism and freedom, with despotism shielded by law, cannot otherwise than demoralize our people. They unsettle the popular mind concerning eternal principles of justice. They harden the heart by familiarity with violence. They accustom people to the idea that it is right for Capital to own Labor; and thus the reverence for Liberty, which we inherited from our fathers, will gradually die out in the souls of our children. We are compelled to disobey our own consciences, and repress all our humane feelings, or else to disobey the law. It is a grievous wrong done to the people to place them between these alternatives. The inevitable result is to destroy the sanctity of law. The doctrine that "might makes right," which our rulers consent to teach the people, in order to pacify slaveholders, will come out in unexpected forms to disturb our own peace and safety. There is "even-handed justice" in the fact that men cannot aid in enslaving others, and themselves remain free; that they cannot assist in robbing others, without endangering their own security.

Moreover, there is wrong done, even to the humblest individual, when he is compelled to be ashamed of his country. When the judge passed under chains into Boston Court House, and when Anthony Burns was sent back into slavery, I wept for my native State, as a daughter weeps for the crimes of a beloved mother. It seemed to me that I would gladly have died to have saved Massachusetts from that sin and that shame. The tears of a secluded woman, who has no vote to give, may appear to you of little consequence. But assuredly it is not well with any Commonwealth, when her daughters weep over her degeneracy and disgrace.

In the name of oppressed humanity, of violated religion, of desecrated law, of tarnished honor, of our own freedom endangered, of the moral sense of our people degraded by these evil influences, I respectfully, but most urgently, entreat you to annul this infamous enactment, so far as the jurisdiction of Massachusetts extends. Our old Commonwealth has been first and foremost in many good works; let her lead in this also. And deem it not presumptuous, if I ask it likewise for my own sake. I am a humble member of the community; but I am deeply interested in the welfare and reputation of my native State, and that gives me some claim to be heard. I am growing old; and on this great question of equal rights I have toiled for years, sometimes with a heart sickened by "hope deferred." I beseech you to let me die on Free Soil! Grant me the satisfaction of saying, ere I go hence—

"Slaves cannot breathe among us. If their lungs Receive our air, that moment they are free! They touch our country, and their shackles fall!"

If you cannot be induced to reform this great wickedness, for the sake of outraged justice and humanity, then do it for the honor of the State, for the political welfare of our own people, for the moral character of our posterity. For, as sure as there is a Righteous Ruler in the heavens, if you continue to be accomplices in violence and fraud, God will not "save the Commonwealth of Massachusetts."

THE DUTY OF DISOBEDIENCE

APPEAL TO THE CONSTITUTIONALITY OF THE FUGITIVE SLAVE ACT

The Hon. Robert Rantoul, Hon. Horace Mann, Hon. Charles Sumner, and other able men, have argued against the Constitutionality of the Fugitive Slave Bill, proving it to be not only contrary to the spirit and meaning of the Constitution, but also to be unauthorized by the letter of that document. That this nefarious Bill is contrary to the spirit and intention of the Constitution is shown by the published opinions of those who framed it; by the debates at the time of its adoption; and by its Preamble, which sets forth that it was ordained to "establish justice, ensure domestic tranquillity, promote the general welfare, and secure the blessings of liberty." The arguments adduced to prove that this bill is unauthorized by the letter of the Constitution, I will endeavor to compress into a few words.

Article 10 of the Amendments to the Constitution expressly provides that "Powers not delegated to the United States by the Constitution, nor prohibited by it to the States, are reserved to the States respectively, or to the people."

Article 4 of the Constitution contains four compacts. The first is:
"Full faith and credit shall be given in each of the States to the public acts, records, and judicial proceedings of every other State. And the Congress may, by general laws, prescribe the manner in which such acts, records and proceedings shall be proved, and the effect thereof."

Here, power is expressly delegated by the Constitution to the United States. The second compact is:
"The citizens of each State shall be entitled to all privileges and immunities of citizens in the several States."

Under this provision, an attempt was made to obtain some action of

Congress for the protection of colored seamen in slaveholding ports; but it was decided that Congress had no power to act on the subject, because the Constitution had not delegated any power to the United States in the clause referred to. Slaveholders are very strict in adherence to the Constitution, whenever any question of protection to colored people is involved in their decisions; but for purposes of oppression, they have no scruples. They reverse the principle of Common Law, that "in any question under the Constitution, every word is to be construed in favor of liberty."

The third compact is:

"A person charged in any State with treason, felony, or other crime, who shall flee from justice, or be found in another State, shall, on demand of the Executive authority of the State from which he fled, be delivered up, to be removed to the State having jurisdiction of the crime."

It has never been pretended that Congress has any power to act in such cases. There is no clause delegating any power to the United States; consequently, all proceedings on the subject have been left to the several States.

The fourth compact is:

"No person held to service or labor in one State, under the laws thereof, escaping into another, shall, in consequence of any law or regulation therein, be discharged from such service or labor, but shall be delivered up on claim of the party to whom such service or labor may be due."

If the framers of the Constitution had meant that Congress should have power to pass a law for delivering up fugitives "held to service or labor," they would have inserted a clause delegating such power, as they did in the compact concerning "public acts and records." The Constitution does not delegate any such power to the United States. Consequently, Congress had no constitutional right to pass the Fugitive Slave Bill, and the States are under no constitutional obligation to obey it.

The Hon. Horace Mann, one of Massachusetts' most honored sons, in his able speech on this subject in Congress, 1851, said:—"In view of the great principles of civil liberty, out of which the Constitution grew, and which it was designed to secure, my own opinion is that this law cannot be fairly and legitimately supported on constitutional grounds. Having formed this opinion with careful deliberation, I am bound to speak from it and to act from it. I have read every argument and every article in defence of the law, from whatever source emanating. Nay, I have been more anxious to read the arguments made in its favor, than the arguments against it; and I think I have seen a sound legal answer to all the former." "It is a law that might be held constitutional by a bench of slaveholders, whose pecuniary interests connect them directly with slavery; or by those who have surrendered themselves to a pro-slavery policy from political hopes. But if we gather the opinions of unbiassed and disinterested men, of those who have no money to make, and no office to hope for, through the triumph of this law, then I think the preponderance of opinion is decidedly against its constitutionality. It is a fact universally known, that gentlemen who have occupied and adorned the highest judicial stations in their respective States, together with many of the ablest lawyers in the whole country, have expressed opinions against the constitutionality of this law." "When I am called upon to support such a law as this, while it lasts, or to desist from opposing it in all constitutional ways, my response is, Repeal the law! that I may no longer be called upon to support it. I demand it, because it is a law which conflicts with the Constitution of the country, and with all the judicial interpretations of that Constitution, wherever they have been applied to the white race. Because it is a law abhorrent to the moral and religious sentiments of a vast majority of the community called upon to enforce it. Because it is a law which, if executed in the Free States, divests them of the character of Free States, and makes them voluntary participators in the guilt of slaveholding. Because it is a law Which disgraces our country in the eyes of the whole civilized world, and gives plausible occasion to the votaries of despotic power to decry republican institutions. Because it is a law which forbids us to do unto others as we would have them do unto us, and which makes it a crime to feed the hungry, to clothe the naked, and to visit and succor the sick and imprisoned. Because it is a law which renders the precepts of the Gospel and the teachings of Jesus Christ seditious; and were the Savior and his band of disciples now on earth, there is but one of them who would escape its penalties by pretending to 'conquer his prejudices.'" "Suppose the whole body of the white population should be as much endangered by this law, as the colored people now are, would the existence of the law be tolerated for an hour? Would there not be a simultaneous and universal uprising of the people against it, and such a yell of execration as never before burst from mortal lips?"

The Hon. Charles Sumner, always true to the right, as the needle to the pole, in his learned and able speech in Congress, 1852, said:—"The true principles of our political system, the history of the National Convention, the natural interpretation of the Constitution, all teach that this Act is a usurpation by Congress of powers that do not belong to it, and an infraction of rights secured to the States. It is a sword, whose handle is at the National Capital, and whose point is every where in the States. A weapon so terrible to personal liberty the nation has no power to grasp." "In the name of the Constitution, which it violates; of my country, which it dishonors; of humanity, which it degrades; of Christianity, which it offends, I arraign this enactment, and now hold it up to the judgment of the Senate and the world."

"The Slave Act violates the Constitution, and shocks the public conscience.

With modesty, and yet with firmness, let me add, it offends against the Divine Law. No such enactment can be entitled to support. As the throne of God is above every earthly throne, so are his laws and statutes above all the laws and statutes of man. To question these, is to question God himself. But to assume that human laws are above question, is to claim for their fallible authors infallibility. To assume that they are always in conformity with those of God, is presumptuously and impiously to exalt man to an equality with God. Clearly, human laws are not always in such conformity; nor can they ever be beyond question from each individual. Where the conflict is open, as if Congress should demand the perpetration of murder, the office of conscience, as final arbiter, is undisputed. But in every conflict, the same queenly office is hers. By no earthly power can she be dethroned. Each person, after anxious examination, without haste, without passion, solemnly for himself must decide this great controversy. Any other rule attributes infallibility to human laws, places them beyond question, and degrades all men to an unthinking, passive obedience. The mandates of an earthly power are to be discussed; those of Heaven must at once be performed; nor can any agreement constrain us against God. Such is the rule of morals. And now the rule is commended to us. The good citizen, as he thinks of the shivering fugitive, guilty of no crime, pursued, hunted down like a beast, while praying for Christian help and deliverance, and as he reads the requirements of this Act, is filled with horror. Here is a despotic mandate, 'to aid and assist in the prompt and efficient execution of this law.' Let me speak frankly. Not rashly would I set myself against any provision of law. This grave responsibility I would not lightly assume. But here the path of duty is clear. By the Supreme Law, which commands me to do no injustice; by the comprehensive Christian Law of Brotherhood; by the Constitution, which I have sworn to support, I am bound to disobey this Act. Never, in any capacity, can I render voluntary aid in its execution. Pains and penalties I will endure; but this great wrong I will not do." "For the sake of peace and tranquillity, cease to shock the public conscience! For the sake of the Constitution, cease to exercise a power which is nowhere granted, and which violates inviolable rights expressly secured. Repeal this enactment! Let its terrors no longer rage through the land. Mindful of the lowly, whom it pursues; mindful of the good men perplexed by its requirements; in the name of charity, in the name of the Constitution, repeal this enactment, totally, and without delay! Be admonished by these words of Oriental piety: 'Beware of the groans of the wounded souls. Oppress not to the utmost a single heart; for a solitary sigh has power to overset a whole world.'"

Robert Rantoul, Jr., whose large heart was so true to Democratic principles, that the party wanted to expel him from their ranks, (as parties are prone to do with honest men,) opposed the Fugitive Slave Bill with all the power of his strong intellect. In a speech delivered in 1851, he said: "I am as devotedly attached as any other man to the Union of these States, and the Constitution of our government; but I admire and love them for that which they secure to us. The Constitution is good, and great, and valuable, and to be held for ever sacred, because it secures to us what was the object of the Constitution. I love the Union and the Constitution, not for themselves, but for the great end for which they were created—to secure and perpetuate liberty; not the liberty of a class, superimposed upon the thraldom of groaning multitudes: not the liberty of a ruling race, cemented by the tears and blood of subject races, but human liberty, perfect liberty, common to the whole people of the United States and to their posterity. It is because I believe all this, that I love the Union and the Constitution. If it were not for that, the Union would be valueless, and the Constitution not worth the parchment on which it is written. God-given Liberty is above the Union, and above the Constitution, and above all the works of man."

TESTIMONIES AGAINST THE FUGITIVE SLAVE ACT

The Hon. Josiah Quincy, senior, whose integrity, noble intellect, and long experience in public life, give great weight to his opinions, made a speech at a Whig Convention in Boston, 1854, from which I extract the following:—
"The circumstances in which the people of Massachusets are placed are undeniably insupportable. What has been seen, what has been felt, by every man, woman and child in this metropolis, and in this community? and virtually by every man, woman and child in Massachusetts? We have seen our Court House in chains, two battalions of dragoons, eight regiments of artillery, twelve companies of infantry, the whole constabulary force of the city police, the entire disposable marine of the United States, with its artillery loaded for action, all marching in support of a Praetorian Band, consisting of one hundred and twenty friends and associates of the U.S. Marshal, with loaded pistols and drawn swords, and in military costume and array; and for what purpose? To escort and conduct a poor trembling slave from a Boston Court House to the fetters and lash of his master!
"This scene, thus awful, thus detestable, every inhabitant of this metropolis, nay, every inhabitant of this Commonwealth, may be compelled again to witness, at any time, and every day in the year, at the will or the whim of the meanest and basest slaveholder of the South. Is there a man in Massachusetts with a spirit so low, so debased, so corrupted by his fears, or his fortune, that he is prepared to say this is a condition of things to be endured in perpetuity by us? and that this is an inheritance to be transmitted by us to our children, for all generations? For so long as the fugitive-slave clause remains in the Constitution, unobliterated, it is an obligation perpetual upon them, as well as upon us.

31

"The obligation incumbent upon the Free States must be obliterated from the Constitution, at every hazard. I believe that, in the nature of things, by the law of God, and the laws of man, that clause is at this moment abrogated, so far as respects common obligation. In 1789, the Free States agreed to be field-drivers and pound-keepers for the Slaveholding States, within the limits, and according to the fences, of the old United States. But between that year and this A.D. 1854, the slaveholders have broken down the old boundaries, and opened new fields, of an unknown and indefinite extent.[1] They have multiplied their slaves by millions, and are every day increasing their numbers, and extending their field into the wilderness. Under these circumstances, are we bound to be their field-drivers and pound-keepers any longer? Answer me, people of Massachusetts! Are you the sons of the men of 1776? Or do you 'lack gall, to make oppression bitter?'

[1] The Hon. Josiah Quincy, while in Congress, always opposed the annexation of foreign territory to the United States, on the ground of its unconstitutionality.

"I have pointed out your burden. I have shown you that it is insupportable. I shall be asked how we are to get rid of it. It is not for a private individual to point the path which a State is to pursue, to cast off an insupportable burden; it belongs to the constituted authorities of that State. But this I will say, that if the people of Massachusetts solemnly adopt, as one man, in the spirit of their fathers, the resolve that they will no longer submit to this burden, and will call upon the Free States to concur in this resolution, and carry it into effect, the burden will be cast off; the fugitive-slave clause will be obliterated, not only without the dissolution of the Union, but with a newly-acquired strength to the Union.".

In the spring of 1860, there was a debate on this subject in the Legislature of New York. In the course of it, Mr. Smith, of Chatauqua, said:—"How came slavery in this country? It came here without law; in violation of all law. It came here by force and violence; by the force of might over right; and it remains here to-day by no better title. And now we are called upon, by the ruling power at Washington, not merely to tolerate it, but to legalize it all over the United States! By the Fugitive Slave Bill, we are forbidden to shelter or assist the forlornest stranger who ever appealed for sympathy or aid. We are required by absolute law to shut out every feeling of compassion for suffering humanity. Fines and imprisonment impend over us, for exercising one of the holiest charities of our religion. Virtue and humanity are legislated into crime. Let us meet the issue like men! Let us assert our utter abhorrence of all human laws, that compel us to violate the common law of humanity and justice; and by so acting assert the broad principles of the Declaration of American Independence, and the letter and spirit of the Constitution. If the North was as devoted to the cause of

Freedom as the South is to Slavery, our national troubles would vanish like darkness before the sun. Our country would then become what it should be,—free, happy, prosperous, and respected by all the world. Then we could say, truthfully, that she is the home of the free, the land of the brave, the asylum of the oppressed."

In the same debate, Mr. Maxson, of Allegheny, said:—"All laws, whether Constitutions or statutes, that invade human rights, are null. A community has no more power to strike down the rights of man by Constitutions, than by any other means. Do those who give us awfully solemn lessons about the inviolability of compacts, mean that one man is bound to rob another because he has agreed to? In this age of schools, of churches and of Bibles, do they mean to teach us that an agreement to rob men of their rights, in whatever solemn form that agreement may be written out, is binding? Has the morality of the nineteenth century culminated in this, that a mere compact can convert vice into virtue? These advocates of the rightfulness of robbery, because it has been agreed, to, and that agreement has been written down, have come too late upon the stage, by more than two hundred years. Where does the proud Empire State wish to be recorded in that great history, which is being so rapidly filled out with the records of this "irrepressible conflict"? For myself, a humble citizen of the State, I ask no prouder record for her than that, in the year 1860, she enacted that the moment a man sets foot on her soil, he is free, against the world!"

Wendell Phillips, one of earth's bravest and best, made a speech at Worcester, 1851, from which I make the following extract:—"Mr. Mann, Mr. Giddings, and other leaders of the Free Soil party, are ready to go to the death against the Fugitive Slave Law. It never should be enforced, they say. It robs men of the jury trial, it robs them of habeas corpus, and forty other things. This is a very good position. But how much comfort would it have been to Ellen Crafts, if she had been sent back to Macon, to know that it had been done with a scrupulous observance of all the forms of habeas corpus and jury trial? When she got back, some excellent friend might have said to her, 'My dear Ellen, you had the blessed privilege of habeas corpus and jury trial. What are you grieving about? You were sent back according to law and the Constitution. What could you want more?' From the statements of our Free Soil friends, you would suppose that the habeas corpus was the great safeguard of a slave's freedom; that it covered him as with an angel's wing. But suppose habeas corpus and jury trial granted, what then? Is any man to be even so surrendered, with our consent? No slave shall be sent back—except by habeas corpus. Stop half short of that! No slave shall be sent back!"

Rev. A.D. Mayo, of Albany, is one of those clergymen who believe that a religious teacher has something to do with questions affecting public morality; and his preaching is eloquent, because he is fearlessly obedient to

his own convictions. In a Sermon on the Fugitive Slave Bill, he said:—
"Remember that despotism has no natural rights on earth that any man is
bound to respect. I know there is no political party, no Christian sect, no
Northern State, as a whole, yet fully up to this. But the Christian sentiment
of the country will finally bring us all to the same conclusion."

NO SLAVE HUNT IN OUR BORDERS!

What asks the Old Dominion? If now her sons have proved
False to their fathers' memory, false to the faith they loved;
If she can scoff at Freedom, and its Great Charter spurn,
Must we of Massachusetts from truth and duty turn?

We hunt your bondmen, flying from Slavery's hateful hell?
Our voices, at your bidding, take up the blood-hound's yell?
We gather, at your summons, above our fathers' graves,
From Freedom's holy altar-horns to tear your wretched slaves?

Thank God! not yet so vilely can Massachusetts bow,
The spirit of her early time is with her even now.
Dream not, because her Pilgrim blood moves slow, and calm, and cool,
She thus can stoop her chainless neck, a sister's slave and tool!

For ourselves and for our children, the vow which we have given
For Freedom and Humanity, is registered in Heaven.
No slave-hunt in our borders! No pirate on our strand!
No fetters in the Bay State! No slave upon our land!
J.G. WHITTIER.

THE HIGHER LAW.

Man was not made for forms, but forms for man;
And there are times when Law itself must bend
To that clear spirit, that hath still outran
The speed of human justice. In the end,
Potentates, not Humanity, must fall.
Water will find its level; fire will burn;
The winds must blow around this earthly ball;
This earthly ball by day and night must turn.
Freedom is typed in every element.
Man must be free! If not through law, why then
Above the law! until its force be spent,
And justice brings a better. When, O, when,

Father of Light! shall the great reckoning come,
To lift the weak, and strike the oppressor dumb?
C.P. CRANCH.

ON THE SURRENDER OF A FUGITIVE SLAVE.

Look on who will in apathy, and stifle, they who can,
The sympathies, the hopes, the words, that make man truly man;
Let those whose hearts are dungeoned up, with interest or with ease,
Consent to hear, with quiet pulse, of loathsome deeds like these.

I first drew in New England's air, and from her hardy breast
Sucked in the tyrant-hating milk, that will not let me rest;
And if my words seem treason to the dullard and the tame,
'Tis but my Bay State dialect—our fathers spake the same.

Shame on the costly mockery of piling stone on stone
To those who won our liberty! the heroes dead and gone!
While we look coldly on and see law-shielded ruffians slay
The men who fain would win their own! the heroes of to-day!

Are we pledged to craven silence? O, fling it to the wind,
The parchment wall that bars us from the least of human kind!
That makes us cringe, and temporize, and dumbly stand at rest,
While Pity's burning flood of words is red-hot in the breast!

We owe allegiance to the State; but deeper, truer, more,
To the sympathies that God hath set within our spirit's core.
Our country claims our fealty; we grant it so; but then
Before Man made us citizens, great Nature made us men!

Though we break our fathers' promise, we have nobler duties first,
The traitor to Humanity is the traitor most accurst.
Man is more than Constitutions. Better rot beneath the sod,
Than be true to Church and State, while we are doubly false to God!
JAMES RUSSELL LOWELL.

STANZAS FOR THE TIMES.

Shall tongues be mute, when deeds are wrought
Which well might shame extremest hell?
Shall freemen lock the indignant thought?
Shall Pity's bosom cease to swell?

Shall Honor bleed? Shall Truth succumb?
Shall pen, and press, and soul be dumb?

What! shall we guard our neighbor still.
While woman shrieks beneath his rod,
And while he tramples down, at will,
The image of a common God?
Shall watch and ward be round him set
Of Northern nerve and bayonet?

And shall we know, and share with him,
The danger and the growing shame?
And see our Freedom's light grow dim,
Which should have filled the world with flame?
And, writhing, feel, where'er we turn,
A world's reproach around us burn?

No! By each spot of haunted ground,
Where Freedom weeps her children's fall;
By Plymouth's rock, and Bunker's mound;
By Griswold's stained and shattered wall;
By Warren's ghost; by Langdon's shade;
By all the memories of our dead;

By their enlarging souls, which burst
The bands and fetters round them set;
By the free Pilgrim spirit, nursed Within our bosoms yet;
By all above, around, below,
Be ours the indignant answer—NO!
J.G. WHITTIER.

VERMONT PERSONAL LIBERTY LAW

AN ACT TO SECURE FREEDOM TO ALL PERSONS WITHIN THIS STATE.

It is hereby enacted, etc.:

Sec. 1. No person within this State shall be considered as property, or subject, as such, to sale, purchase, or delivery; nor shall any person, within the limits of this State, at this time, be deprived of liberty or property without due process of law.

Sec. 2. Due process of law, mentioned in the preceding section of this Act shall, in all cases, be defined to mean the usual process and forms in force by the laws of this State, and issued by the courts thereof; and under such process, such person shall be entitled to a trial by jury.

Sec. 3. Whenever any person in this State shall be deprived of liberty, arrested, or detained, on the ground that such person owes service or labor to another person, not an inhabitant of this State, either party may claim a trial by jury; and, in such case, challenges shall be allowed to the defendant agreeably to sections four and five of chapter one hundred and eleven of the compiled statutes.

Sec. 4. Every person who shall deprive or attempt to deprive any other person of his or her liberty, contrary to the preceding sections of this Act, shall, on conviction thereof, forfeit and pay a fine not exceeding two thousand dollars nor less than five hundred dollars, or be punished by imprisonment in the State Prison for a term not exceeding ten years: Provided, that nothing in said preceding sections shall apply to, or affect the right to arrest or imprison under existing laws for contempt of court.

Sec. 5. Neither descent near or remote from an African, whether such African is or may have been a slave or not, nor color of skin or complexion, shall disqualify any person from being, or prevent any person from becoming, a citizen of this State, nor deprive such person of the rights and privileges thereof.

Sec. 6. Every person who may have been held as a slave, who shall come, or be brought, or be in this State, with or without the consent of his or her master or mistress, or who shall come, or be brought, or be, involuntarily or in any way in this State, shall be free.

Sec. 7. Every person who shall hold, or attempt to hold, in this State, in slavery, or as a slave, any person mentioned as a slave in the sixth section of this act, or any free person, in any form, or for any time, however short, under pretence that such person is or has been a slave, shall, on conviction thereof, be imprisoned in the State Prison for a term not less than one year, nor more than fifteen years, and be fined not exceeding two thousand dollars.

Sec. 8. All Acts and parts of Acts inconsistent with the provisions of this Act are hereby repealed.

Sec. 9. This Act shall take effect from its passage.

Approved November 25, 1858.

www.ingramcontent.com/pod-product-compliance
Lightning Source LLC
Chambersburg PA
CBHW070513290526
45790CB00003B/1222